GW00671282

Gallery Books
Editor: Peter Fallon

CRY FOR THE HOT BELLY

Kerry Hardie

CRY FOR THE HOT BELLY

4/7/0r

Ann —

with love

— Kerry

Gallery Books

Cry for the Hot Belly
is first published
simultaneously in paperback
and in a clothbound edition
on 11 May 2000.

The Gallery Press
Loughcrew
Oldcastle
County Meath
Ireland

© Kerry Hardie 2000

ISBN 1 85235 265 5 (*paperback*)
      1 85235 266 3 (*clothbound*)

The Gallery Press acknowledges the financial assistance
of An Chomhairle Ealaíon / The Arts Council, Ireland,
and the Arts Council of Northern Ireland.

Contents

for Paddy and Dorothy

Prayer Flags

Make flags,
write on them,
hoist them into blue air.

Never let songs
of dream or prayer
stay earthbound, unsung.

Old Men, the Maps in their Heads

The celandines in the grass,
the crows in the empty ash —
its swooping buds on the sky.

In this white time of Spring
they walk the roads like men
drowned yet not knowing it.

Watching them seeing
things seen for years:
their meticulous, still attention —

watching them watching
the cross-hatch of roads, the scatter of fields,
as men who will leave them —

I feel to a denser map
than those patterns of lines and names
that cartographers leak onto paper.

Kitchen Work

The potatoes peel yellow under my fingers,
they splash into the white bowl.

If I stabbed my finger with the paring knife
the colour-seep on the wet flesh of the skinned potato
could be swatched from the crimson dress
that hangs on the stained plaster wall
in the dream that I dreamed last night
that leaves day the paler.

Intimacy

When it had rained all day and all night
the sea was yellow with bog water,
brown and green leaves floated there;
twigs, seedheads and grey feathers.

I walked in it, all those hours,
the dog swimming beside me like an otter,
my mind scoured clean by the fine sea-grit,
thoughts as puffs of sand from the sea's floor.

The salmon that hung in the shallows the day before
were all gone up the river with the rains,
and in the dunes the cerise of the pyramidal orchids
lay beside the yellow bedstraw and the uncombed marram
    grass;

shells and the legs and armoured backs of crabs
were scattered like seed, the pointed tern shrieked in the
    sky.
I had five small stones of purple slate
laid on my opened palm for him.

I had placed them, intending an offering,
but my hand kept its distance. I only showed them.
Then I caught, with the corner of my eye,
the stones on the blue quilt of the rented holiday bed

and I knew they were the self-stones, deepening all colours;
they must be kept clean and held separate.

Connemara Easter

for Jen and Ron Bain

The things we saw that day:
the wide bog, planted with flags like broad-swords
growing in blue-green ranks where the eye ran;
the seals in the cove, the hare in the uplands,
the turn of an otter's back in the swell of a wave;
the diver out in the bay, how it rolled over
and preened its white belly and you said
in North America it's called a loon, it's on the stamps.
Then we walked on over the dune-sands
studded with shells and slivers of bone
and star-like plants as in a *mille-fleurs* tapestry.

What we carried back with us
into the place where stone became thorn hedges,
where the wild cherry stood in the still of the evening,
and the opened boots of cars on the road home
held harrows and lawnmowers and bales of hay;
what we carried back was a secret.
The white strand, the frail colour of the sea moving over it,
the spring day running out, the empty sands,
the otter's clawmarks, leisurely, a rolling trot,
going into the wash, not coming back, leaving
a small deep awe, kin to strewn grave-cloths.

Bachelors

I could live on any hillside in Ireland
in this white light with the wild cherry blowing,
I could belong
anywhere.

I would drive the roads,
watch the old men standing,
their following eyes asking
whose daughter are you?

I would be the right age for a daughter,
for them to catch a likeness,
something familiar
in the turn of the head.

I would see then their remembering
of young women dwelling off small roads
in these same grassy townlands
years ago.

Girls courted
and then walked away from for no final reason
just some petulance
of the blood,

or because the evening was so blue and distant
as to leave that blood no choice but wandering;
and soon the grass grew high
and all the girls were gone to other houses.

I would come from anywhere,
be any woman's daughter,
so I might borrow grace from old men's eyes
along these haunted roadsides in the Spring.

She Replies to Carmel's Letter

It was a mild Christmas, the small fine rain kept washing
    over,
so I coated myself in plastics,
walked further than I could manage.
Leave me now, I'd say, and when they had tramped ahead
I'd sit myself down on a stone or the side of a high grass
    ditch,
or anywhere — like a duck in a puddle —
I'd rest a bit, then I would muddle around
the winding boreens that crawled the headland.

Sometimes, water-proofed and not caring,
I'd sit in a road which was really a stream-bed,
being and seeing from down where the hare sees,
sitting in mud and in wetness,
the world rising hummocky round me,
the sudden grass on the skyline,
the fence-post, with the earth run from under it,
swinging like a hanged man.

Then I would want to praise
the ease of low wet things, the song of them, like a child's
    low drone,
and praising I'd watch how the water flowing the track
is clear, so I might not see it
but for the cross-hatched place where it runs on a scatter
    of grit,
the flat, swelled place where it slides itself over a stone.
So now, when you write that you labour to strip off the
    layers,
and there might not, under them, be anything at all,

I remember that time, and I wish you had sat there, with
   me,
your skin fever-hot, the lovely wet coldness of winter mud
on your red, uncovered hands,
knowing it's all in the layers,
the flesh on the bones, the patterns that the bones push
upwards onto the flesh. So, you will see how it is with me,
and that sometimes even sickness is generous
and takes you by the hand and sits you
beside things you would otherwise have passed over.

Vitality

for Victor and Rachel

'Tell her to use the pool. Swimming will make her stronger.'

All winter I slipped between its blue sheets, I moved
through the lucent space that did not resist me.
The low day lapped at the windows, the blue rectangle
printed itself on my dreams.
No one but me. I saw snow-fade, light-stretch,
sun-quiver on the pool's blue floor.
Got stronger,
grew
lonely.

          ᕤ

He told me of a market where they went
to buy blue carp at Christmas when they lived in Prague.

He said in Prague there was an outdoor pool,
you lowered yourself down ladders hung with ice,
you slid beneath white steam that hid the stars.
Arthritics liked to swim there,
and people like them, without baths.
The snow lay banked beside the walkways.
It glittered like salt.

          ᕤ

The yellowed tiles, the knots and veins,
the scabby unwashed forms.
The inky flicker of a blue carp's tail.

I looked out from my life
and it was silk-thin and too easily torn.

The Cruellest Month

for Bernadette Kiely

We came round the bent road in the drowned light
of a Spring evening
and I saw you, in your dark coat,
your hair dark, your face white, your hands full of lilacs —

You might have been a bride, the way you walked,
your head high, him beside you, but separate,
like a woman coming from the church a hundred years ago,
going home with the man, to begin the life contracted.

It was all lit
from elsewhere: the stormy evening, the white light,
the small squat houses, the river running black
by the stone quays, the chestnuts climbing.

And those lilacs, a mass of them,
spreading out of your hands:
a white one, a mauve one, a white one —
Not casual. Some eye deciding, some hand arranging
the eye's bidding.

All week I'd been on about lilacs,
had stood by a window in the evening looking down
on a lilac in the garden, its few blooms
with the reddish stain of blood behind their purple —

Those famous lines were in my mind, this being the month,
but it wasn't right — his lilacs, not our lilacs.
Our lilacs: out of a green land, some with blood on their
    roots.
And white ones, planted by the Marian grottos.
And mauve, plebeian, by the ruined gable ends.

These lilacs, drawn to your hands
like the thought-forms of flowers;
their fall over your hands, down the dark coat,
their thick scent on the chilly air.

You, by the quay, walking another century,
as though our dramas act and re-enact on the same stage,
so that I saw you,
and a woman that had gone before you,
and lilacs, clustering into your hands from hers.

Vera in May

i.m. Vera Middleton 1951-1998

This time of year
countrywomen put on cotton blouses:
mostly white or blue or sprigged with flowers.

This time of year
the beech put on full leaf:
fresh and ancient where the light shines through.

This time of year
I praise the lucent world, its incarnation:
cow parsley nets ditches with fresh lace.

This year, this time of year,
Vera lies dying: fitting the blouse,
its loose folds that the light shines through.

Stranger

He thinks that bearded iris
is female, nineteenth century.
He doesn't know why.
I think he is thinking of systems of mourning:
of women in black for years, then in full purple,
of fringes and beadwork and brooches displaying
coils of gold hair looped into fleurs-de-lis.

I don't see it like that, unless it's Wilde —
the same exotic and ungainly body —
I see it eighteenth century, androgynous,
its stiff buds and bearded lip,
its mauve crown-petals open to receive.

The way I see it, the way he sees it —
neither able to handle
its odd and stately presence in the long bed,
this sense of something complex and evolved
inhabiting our green untidy acre,
while all the fields beyond
are high with grasses flowering into hay.

Fuller's Earth

for Maeve Malley

I saw at last
that she was made from silvery shale,
that if you rubbed her with your finger

flakes might fall,
all shimmery with bright dust;
that she was set

on being less and less substantial,
trying to change from flesh
and into something

blind and blundering,
night-flying,
differently attuned.

Soft, thickened wings
of taupe, the body
furred in cinnamon,

eyes black and huge as night
where she'd grow fluent
till it was as day.

Dog-Daisies

i.m. Dermot Keith Goodwillie 1975-1997

'Better today,' his mother said on the phone. 'Yesterday
I wanted desperately for there to be a baby.
I knew it wouldn't be him, but I wanted some part of him.
Roger said I was silly, how would we manage?
We had a whole long talk about the problem,
Then Caoimhe came, her arms full of dog-daisies.'
The rain comes, the rain goes,
there never was a year like this for dog-daisies.

Her funeral skirt floated with poppies,
his father wore a summer suit and they smiled
and kissed everyone. Everyone wept.
His sister smiled, the young people smiled,
their mouths quivered,
the reading was from Catcher in the Rye.
The light kept changing,
the rain came, the rain went,
and what a year it was for dog-daisies.

Burying him
felt like the giving back of the best, as in a sacrifice:
the sweetest well, the greenest flowering meadow.
It was hard to give thanks for a life, as they did,
with the June trees in the wind, their leaves shivering,
the elderflower full out, its scent on the wet air —
To let him go into the ground was hard.
The light changes, the rain comes,
and never such a year for dog-daisies.

Monaghan Solstice

Sunlight — a window
in the week's rain.
Eight sparrows bathe
in the dust of the broken road.
Black and white cows pull the lush grass.
A yellow bull saunters; swallows skim.

The sloping fields are loud with the sound
of grass lying down to the blade —
it's half-way dry, the rain's holding off —
no one about but the land,
surging and hummocky
as the sea.

On such a day
Persephone was seized,
(no one about, land like the sea,
dog roses, guelder rose, that ochre bull,
those ink-blue swallows with their warm, stained chests).

Persephone being seized, the bright world stilled.

So what's to be done now but stand,
foxgloves tall in the ditches?
Watching things ceasing,
becoming the next thing.
Heart quiet,
world turning.

Exiles

1

This is a work of remembrance, the remembrance of lives.
And of times. Of land, water, sky.
Sometimes there are only the names and the lives are lost;
sometimes there are only the lives and the names are lost.
To remember, in a time of forgetting.

I was standing on spread newspapers,
an altar vase locked under my arm,
my hand's warmth misting its yellow brass,
pulling at the flowers in it, stiff and still fresh,
although it was ten days from Christmas —
and Nancy, beside me in the frozen church,
saying she had Irish in her.

They came away in a mass, their stems embedded,
I had to stamp on them to break the ice
to free out ivy that I wanted for the funeral vases.

My mother-in-law was coming in her coffin
to lie in the stone-dark through the Northern night.
And none of us minded that —
not the coldness nor the sweep of the wind —
because she'd always liked outside, all-weather,
and the next day she would move off, we would follow after
to stand while she took the place prepared for her
in the slit earth in the grey bowl of the hills.

Nancy said it was her father that had made her love the
    music.
Her father was half-Irish; his father had been Irish.

She was trying to make me understand
but I was thinking of flowers
and I didn't. *My father was illegitimate.*
The hardness of the old word focused me.
Her grandfather's name — Sheridan — was on the
    Certificate.
He had come here, but she didn't know why.
Then he had gone away again.

No, she answered me, he hadn't let her down.
He would have married her, her people wouldn't have him.
They sent him off. But they kept his child.

Nancy was telling me this, her eyes bright, fresh,
everything direct, her voice lifting, falling with the Northern
    vowels,
her face young, and there was nothing ever that need be
    hidden
or avoided. She was a shepherd's wife, for forty years
they'd kept a farm on the high moors,
had watched the weather build over Scotland,
the rim of light edging the rise of the land,
the clean rain hanging from the pointed grasses.

She hadn't known my mother-in-law to talk to, only by
    sight.
I thought to say to Nancy, she was Irish too,
although she had the accent of an English lady;
I nearly said it but I didn't,
I wanted to leave Nancy with her Irish grandfather
who had come there and gone away again,
whose name had been Sheridan,
who was likely as not a labourer or a drover.

2

At my feet were florist's bunches:
tiger lilies, spray chrysanthemums.
I wanted holly for its shiny darkness,
so I could drown the florist's flowers in it,
so I could take her back to her beginnings,
which was where she had taken herself through the
    Alzheimer's.
I wanted her to lie there in the frozen darkness,
unharrassed by tiger lilies or chrysanthemums.
My husband, her youngest son, went out into the fading
    light
and cut long spears of holly from the churchyard,
and I broke the stems and thrust them
into the mouths of the vases, brassy as cymbals.

And Nancy said to leave the spent flowers and the bits of
    stem
because it was her turn for cleaning and she loved the
    music —
the fiddles and the pipes. I saw him then, her Irish grand-
    father,
his back turned, tramping away,
over those bleak moors which pulse with larks in summer.

3

She died in the deep of winter
when the cattle break out of the empty fields
when the earth has split open in darkness
and the white mist pours its breath into the night.

On her coffin, only the name she took when she was
  married.
Gone, all of her life before that ceremonial crossing,
all her crowded ancestors are shooed away,
no point them to come peering
over the rim of the darkness like so many gargoyles,
they'll get no satisfaction here, nor any welcome.
Nor would she have wanted them in her lucid days,
but after things started colliding and sliding away
the landscape was all changed and changed
and even her husband of sixty years didn't know its
  contours.
None could say where she roamed nor whom she lived
  with.
All we were sure of was it was not us.

4

In Ireland a man must have a home town,
somewhere to leave behind him, somewhere to long to
    return to.
A woman makes her home town in her children.
In them she makes her claim, in them is her belonging.

Shelagh Jacob was her name.
She has gone into the dark with all the rest of them
and it is 'Nobody's funeral, for there is no one to bury.'
Ah, but there is, there's a husk in a box and all us live ones
waiting to bear witness to a womb
that spewed new generations for the dark.

He, leaving his name, losing his child.
She, losing her name, leaving children.
And what she liked and what she didn't like
is only personality. And the live children that she bore
are only issue. Her one dead child
is only suffering. And there is nothing to lose
for it is all already gone.

5

We stand in the frozen grass;
the skeins of geese fly over —
dissolving, reforming,
thinning out like stitches on leather,
bunching close, like strung beads.

6

The flight home was delayed and we waited, bone tired. I thought of Dublin and the long drive home through the softer, darker Irish night; of how in the morning we would wake in our own place with its small blue mountains and its tangled fields, far from this country of moors and high fells and rapid broken streams.

I thought of the man Sheridan, his boots and his stick.

7

And now it is near to the solstice again.
The old man, her husband, is dying.
Slowly. The body, taking its time.
And evening after evening, all through the year
after the urgent work, I have sat with this piece,
trying to understand; failing.
And all I have left is remembrance,
frail and wavering as dream.

This is a work of remembrance, the remembrance of lives.
And of times. Of land, water, sky.
Sometimes there are only the names and the lives are lost,
sometimes there are only the lives and the names are lost.
To remember, in a time of forgetting.
In the long wail of the pipes, the language of remembrance,
and Nancy, her clear eyes looking ahead,
her yearning and remembrance in the music.

Signals

A morning of swift grey skies,
crows walking the wet roads.

Then, just before Carlow,
a field got up and took to the air:
white-bellied birds, their dark, splayed wings
flopping up into the sky.

In the night I had woken
to this new cold, draping my shoulders.
The hand, plunged deeper into the black pool.
Now, here were the lapwings
rising up from the rushy field;
lapwings, flying out of the north,
filling the skies with their old, fierce weather.

And what can we do
but what must be done,
no matter what is lost or left behind us?

And I knew there'd be more flocks on the skyline
when we reached the bleak, wide flatlands of Kildare.

A Family Affair

I REALMS

The old man could not any longer lift his legs.
And he had so many dreams.
Was it any wonder
he left off shuffling out of them?

We tried to go there — into his dreams — but the way was
    barred.
Not by him —
he would have had us enter and walk with him —
by the daylight we carried, our hands reverent.

2 BEFORE THE BURIAL: SPEAKING TO KATIE

I have been in this church before, it is not the church
we buried his mother from; it is the church
we married my niece, your daughter, from.
And the time I came before was on a June evening
when we walked in from our journey and you were here,
hunkered on the floor, gathering into newspapers
bits of torn leaf and stem, your arms spread
like a woman in a pietà, the same tenderness in your face.
You had been placing flowers in bowls and jugs
against the wedding of your daughter the next morning.

3 AFTER THE BURIAL: SPEAKING TO KATIE

It is not that I think a man must do this, a woman that.
I am interested in the sacred that we do for each other,
in the privacy and definition of these tasks,
in how their wrought-ness acts upon us.
I am interested in androgyny,
in the strengthening
of the man in me and the woman in me,
in these beings walking forward to face trials
that will render them more subtle and sweet, one to another,
closer to silence.

Bird Trees

for Eileen and John

Two blackbirds, a mistle thrush,
its finger-painted chest,
in the almost leafless
malus japonica, a small tree
with a lacquered name,
grey on grey light.

Once I had a picture
of an Indian Bird Tree:
green on green ground
crusted with birds —
thin, black-beaked crows, more all the time,
winging in, winging out.

My mind called it
a mulberry tree,
not knowing much about mulberries;
only about spindleberries, haws
and long bright hips;
the guelder rose — its luminous spheres.

Local fruits. And Sweeney's birds
in the leafless cage
of the branched tree. Songbirds.
And my life there,
mouse-small,
my heart an open leafless cage

in the grey light with sometimes
birds in it. Far from
the Indian Bird Tree:
green on green ground,
great heat, black birds,
winging out, winging in.

Detail of Disintegration*

There's Degas' little Dancer — her bronze head, bronze hips,
bronze feet. And sprouting from the bodice of her tutu — her
bronze-net skirt.

You have to look a second time, the colour's so exact. It
might be netting cast in bronze, not net, bronze-dyed. You
look a second time. You think: a lovely detail; so feminine a
gesture from a man. You are all pleasure.

You walk around the case to see her back — the bronze
plait centring it. You find the plait is tied with satin ribbon
that is buttermilk-coloured, real as day. Already limpening,
flopping.

It's not feminine, this second gesture — it's beyond all that.

Satin. You know that no glass case or temperature-control
can save it; can stop it from gradually losing itself, from
becoming no more than a fall of dust down the bronze back.

An arc, like spoor, at the bronze feet.

You think of Degas, sculptor, working out of flesh that,
like the satin ribbon, can't be stopped. You wonder if he tied
the ribbon for his own flesh's sake.

*On seeing Degas' 'Dancer' in the Tate Gallery, London

Seal Morning

The small seal, laid on the greyish sand
like a bolster — the same off-white colour —
its smooth, tight, belly-ticking holed by a crow,
one thick thread of blackened entrail
pulled out and looped loosely over its body.
And the crow — standing off — waiting.

Like those old stories of the Vikings,
how they'd prick a man's belly and hook out
a coil of his gut. Then they'd nail it to a tree
and make him crawl round and around,
unwinding himself, the tree taking his entrails,
as a bobbin draws thread from a spool.

The sea mist was a blowing whiteness,
the small seal lay on its back in a curve,
one flipper folded across its body,
the other outstretched. Like a sunbather
lying in easy abandon, asleep. Too private really;
too like someone at rest in their own bed.

The pale-grey spots of its markings
just showed through the white belly-bristle,
and on the sands were blooms of flattened weed
and gutted crabs and broken shells
and the long line
of the small, low waves, running in.

It was like those Impressionist views
of beaches in Northern France
in the white, morning light —
the people strolling in pale clothes,
the navy ribbons on the boaters flapping,
the sun, trying to break through.

The crow stood on the tide-stretched strand,
surveying its handiwork.
Attentive, but also indifferent.
Like the Vikings.
Like the painter
when the whitish light is in the painting.

An Ancient Practice

On wet days
to sit licking at pain

(tongue tentative
as fingers in the dark)

to find its blue outline
and comfort the flesh in its travails.

Covenant

The grid of ribbed light sliding under the water
as the full tide slides into the little stream-cut creeks.
The blue rib of the storm-broken boat.

ᨳ

The high arching of ribs over the slack belly
of the dun cow lain on the rushy grass
in the washed morning light, the storm spent.

ᨳ

The ribbed arc of sprung bone
of the fish on the river path,
the belly eaten away, the ribs rising to shield it.

ᨳ

How the ribs rise everywhere
over the hot, soft belly;
how I, seeing everywhere,
high life collapsing into death,

walk here by the black-plumed reed
ribbed with the purple of loosestrife,
cry for the hot belly
gone from the bleaching bone.

Carthage

Lying beside you,
my hand on your sleeping,
feeling your life,
a pulse of light round the skin.

Lying beside you,
your strong bones, dense flesh.
This life-thing. No more than the weight
of a blink of the moth's eye.

Washing

I remember that gaunt house,
mud to the door,
filled crack in the gable end,
work-clothes on the line (dark, weighty, shapeless),
the sound of water running
through gaps and dripping places,
down the shine of the road,
seeping among the rushes.
Then the gleam of wet roof-slates
in the hopelessly radiant light,
and the rose-coloured nightdress,
loud as a birth,
hung with those drab vestments —
it's a woman farms that land —
Her tender life
moves in the wet wind against the mountain.

Summer's End

for John Fortune

A wind from the south
bowls the last of the summer before it.
The hollyhocks lie out on the wet grass,
their still-opening flowers of sodden pink crêpe
nose-down in the dew. Already they are gone
beyond themselves. The white dress adorns
the pregnant bride.
                    The blue colour
is on mountains, meadows, distances. The harvest
is being brought in.
                    The air birds — swallows and martins —
are blowing all over the sky which has stretched and stretched
like Leonardo's man, describing his full circle.
The earth has grown smaller and denser,
the tight-packed muscle of the diaphragm
hoarding its power.
The trees lift their burdened branches
up into the windy, white sky
like souls that crave nakedness.
                    There is an urgency
in the warm wind, a new vigour. Like a man
in late middle age, who, waking one morning,
knows his fate: sees
the smoke-hues lick under the brightness;
the flowers, taking garment of fire and of shadow.
These sombre washes, tightening the world,
sweetening its dark honey.

'Wherever There is Ruin, There is Hope for Treasure'
— Jalaluddin Rumi, d. 1273

for Eilish Martin

To see you advancing —
dogged, resolute, perfectly conscious —

while I
was always unsteady,
always loved
the rumpled bed.

To see you
plodding
forward into moonless darkness

while I
always hold out
for some amelioration
of the situation, even it's only
starlight, a shine of white frost —

When I think
how I mince and skitter
how my eyes roll and my head rears

while you
don't even bother
to look up.

༄

Sometimes shame
steadies me. Sometimes
fear.

Were I to succeed in avoiding

what I'm trying so desperately
to avoid
it would, in the long run,
prove fatal.

To be carrying on
like this,
though the darkness pours
all around —

The Bread We Live By

for Anne and Kathleen

In the lit room, three women talking,
the curtains open, night at the window,
the big leaves
blowing out of the darkness like pale birds,
batting against the glass;
the women looking up
from their talk, which is quiet and warm, a worn hand
on a washed cloth; looking up
at the soft frap of the leaves — attentive —
coming back, the voices steady
in the steady, everyday electric light,
pausing again at the pale birds' rush,
at their loose, blown voyaging through night.

Harvest

You, being farm-reared,
write of grain filling the red barn.

For me it's in the bales they're carrying home,
the hedges fluttering straw, the brown-armed men.

Autumn's Fall

It seems the rain will be its end — the smell
of rotting-down in ditches, under trees,
the sharp scent of late apples in wet grass,
the spent leaves guttering in the stone-flagged well.

The spaces in the branches stretch and grow.
High spiralling of crows in the thin sky.
The grey drift of the distance. Nothing more
of hope or exultation in the flow

of damp air from the windows that I leave
to let the year move quietly through the house
preparing for the long dark and the cold,
loosening the nets spent thoughts still weave,

clingy as cobwebs. There must be space for death,
and witness for this seep of emptying light;
for winter, pressing with the cattle at the gate,
clouding the darkness with their frightened breath.

The Heart's Adultery

for Katie

She showed me the frosted tufts
of the winter barley,
the stalks cut square and close
where the geese had grazed.

She showed me a rheumy eye
in the iron meadow,
the growth-rings in its ice
like marks in a cut tree.

She said when the hoar frosts came
the hairs on the cattle
stood shining and separate.
The thorns glittered.

She said when he was away
she came here at first light
before the land was up.
She'd seen its intimate
and hidden self.

❧

The land lay all around
like an opened hand.
The sky leaned down
and laid its face there.

Animals and Snow

The rabbit tracks in the snow
on the high field in the morning.
The great white field
criss-crossed under a sky
thick with the coming snow.

The fine snow, falling and falling.
The small *phut phut*
of snow on his gabardine coat.
The muffled empty sound
of white distance.

The horses, trudging the snow;
him standing, arm held out,
a winter-shrunken apple on the palm,
waiting for the colts
to stretch their long necks and feed.

The black horse, lipping the fruit
that rolls off into the snow.
Him, placing another. The black horse
has it; the chestnut takes the next,
the bay can't fetch up courage.

Behind them a fox
quits the stone barn,
soundlessly crosses the field.
There's another. Smaller, redder —
she trots white space.

Then the apples are gone,
the foxes are gone;
the bay walks behind,
its swinging gait
forlorn against the snow

which is like grace,
like the beginning,
so it is easy to think
of a young world running with beasts,
beautiful and furred and dark.

Things That are Lost

My mother teaches me the fading skills:
how to clean fish, plait garlic, draw pheasants;
how to distinguish wading birds,
how to make linen lace.

I know her ache because it is in me.
I try to teach to anyone who'll listen
wild flowers: their legends, properties, names.
I do this in full love of the fresh world.

But a voice says,
Lose things, forget them, let them go.
See all things always the first time.
Unnamed. In wonder.

Mother, in Age

like weather that's always
busy about the place, filling
the long pond, warming
the near pavement, feathering
grasses in the upper field —

Now she has stripped the leaves,
she has ice-flowered
the water in the barrel, and I
wind my horn through her falling snow
against the hushed stillness

of its lying.

What's Left

for Peter Hennessy

I used to wait for the flowers,
my pleasure reposed on them.
Now I like plants before they get to the blossom.
Leafy ones — foxgloves, comfrey, delphiniums —
fleshy tiers of strong leaves pushing up
into air grown daily lighter and more sheened
with bright dust like the eyeshadow
that tall young woman in the bookshop wears,
its shimmer and crumble on her white lids.

The washing sways on the line, the sparrows pull
at the heaps of drying weeds that I've left around.
Perhaps this is middle age. Untidy, unfinished,
knowing there'll never be time now to finish,
liking the plants — their strong lives —
not caring about flowers, sitting in weeds
to write things down, look at things,
watching the sway of shirts on the line,
the cloth filtering light.

I know more or less
how to live through my life now.
But I want to know how to live what's left
with my eyes open and my hands open;
I want to stand at the door in the rain
listening, sniffing, gaping.
Fearful and joyous,
like an idiot before God.

Fire-Tulips

I am punching holes in a dark cloth,
planting bulbs in pocks fast filling with the night,
setting flares in the dusk.

When Spring comes I shan't care,
they'll be tulips in a garden full of easy colours
in the easy light; I shan't care
anymore than for a dress I wanted desperately last year —

But tonight it's sodden, rotten —
I grub in five o'clock November night and watch
red tulips burning, burning in the navy garden.

That Old Song

Because it is so lovely —
the wind sweeping the poplars,
the cloudy darkness gathering
bluish over the high whitethorn,
their burden of blossom as though sliding
from off their stiff branches
into dim grass.

Us too, our living sliding from us —
creamy, fragrant, and discarded —
so it seems easy to unfetter,
easy to move upwards
in the slow dusk of late May, early June.
And I, thinking: I don't have to remember or hold on,
I live this now, it is deep in the life.

Acknowledgements

Acknowledgements are due to the editors and publishers of *At the Year's Turning* (Dedalus), *College Green*, *Cúirt Journal*, *HU*, *Irish University Review*, *New Writer*, *Peterloo Poster*, *Poetry Ireland Review*, *Poetry Now* (Dun Laoghaire/Rathdown), *Ropes*, *Stroan*, *Tabla*, *Verse* and *Works*.

'She Replies to Carmel's Letter' won first prize in the Poetry Ireland Friends Provident/National Poetry Competition (1996) and was published in *Poetry Ireland Review*. 'Exiles' won first prize in the Phras Competition (1997) and was published in the *Phras Anthology*.

Thanks are due to the Tyrone Guthrie Centre at Annaghmakerrig.

The author wishes particularly to thank all at Butler House.